a bit on the side

Miriam Elshaikh

Angus&Robertson
An imprint of HarperCollins*Publishers*

For my mother Amaline, who taught and inspired me in the kitchen, and today inspires me in my life. I would like to acknowledge the unconditional love, help and support of my family and close friends with whom I've shared many culinary adventures, in places ranging from campfires to Newtown! In particular, thanks to Najet, Abe, Robyn, Stephen, Bill, Bridget, Wendy and Diane for helping to make this book a reality. I would also like to thank my late father, Mahmoud, who, along with my mother, helped to awaken in me a deep appreciation of my culture.

An Angus&Robertson Publication

Angus&Robertson, an imprint of HarperCollins *Publishers*
25–31 Ryde Road, Pymble, NSW 2073, Australia
31 View Road, Glenfield, Auckland 10, New Zealand
77–85 Fulham Palace Road, London W6 8JB, United Kingdom
10 East 53rd Street, New York NY 10022, USA

First published in Australia in 1995

National Library of Australia
Cataloguing-in-publication data:

Elshaikh, Miriam, 1954-
    A bit on the side.
    ISBN 0207 184232
    1. Condiments. 2. Side dishes (Cookery). I Title.
641.81

Photography by Brett Odgers
Design by Robyn Latimer
Printed in Hong Kong

98 97 96 95
5 4 3 2 1

Contents

introduction iv

dips and sauces 1

Eggplant and Yoghurt Dip 2

Houmous (Chickpea Dip) 3

Cucumber and Yoghurt 4

Baba Ganouj (Eggplant Dip) 6

Indonesian Onion Sauce 8

Tahini and Garlic Sauce 9

Seeded Mustard with Fresh Herbs 10

Toum (Garlic Paste) 12

Home-made Yoghurt 13

vegetables, salads and rice 15

Spicy Green Beans 16

Spicy Potatoes 17

Garlic and Lemon Snake Beans 18

Beetroot Salad 20

Oregano and Onion Salad 21

Roasted Capsicum 22

Roasted Banana Chillies 23

Leeks Vinaigrette 25

Dried Tomatoes 26

Tomato, Onion & Coriander Salad 27

Tabbouli (Parsley Salad) 28

Marinated Zucchinis 29

Chickpea Salad 31

Pilau with Pine Nuts & Raisins 32

pickles and chutneys 35

Choko Pickles 36

Stuffed Pickled Baby Eggplants 37

Mint and Coriander Chutney 39

Home-made Preserved Olives 40

Marinated Olives 41

Pickled Vegetables 42

oils, vinegars, dressings and marinades 45

Herb Vinegars 47

Herb Oils 48

Mustard Salad Dressing 50

Vinaigrette Salad Dressing 50

Greek-style Marinade 51

Tandoori Marinade 53

Asian-style Marinade 54

introduction

Influences from other countries have given us new ingredients, new tastes, and generally a new approach to the way we present a meal. While meat, fish or poultry is often still the main focus, vegetables, salads, and condiments — grouped together as accompaniments or the 'bit on the side' — have taken on a life of their own. In fact, these days, some can be served as a meal in their own right, something like the concept of Italian 'antipasto'.

While these recipes offer suggestions of 'things to go with things', I would encourage the cook to try an array of these recipes served in buffet-style, for example, at a summer evening gathering, a vegetarian brunch or a picnic lunch. Whatever the occasion, many of them can stand alone as tasty, interesting, and sometimes unusual dishes.

My cultural background, which is Middle Eastern, has been the foundation for my interest and experience in cooking food, particularly food from that region. Young girls are encouraged, practically from their mother's breast, to take part in the preparation of food, whether it be turning the handle of the bench mincer, making miniature, slightly misshapen versions of Mum's more uniformly-shaped stuffed kibbe (spicy minced lamb parcels), or tasting the cabbage rolls to see if the rice stuffing is cooked. The training ground for women from my culture begins at Mum's elbow during preparation, and follows her through to the serving of the meal. Albeit slightly 'underfoot', Mum made sure I did not miss a step — all the way to the washing up!

While, initially, my culinary experiences were mainly traditional Middle Eastern, my interests and experiments broadened to include foods from farther afield. Some recipes I have changed and adapted to suit my own expanding tastes and those of my dear, supportive and often hungry friends; however, some are tried and true recipes handed down from mother to daughter long before I was the proverbial 'twinkle in my mother's eye'.

The recipes in this book are a collection of the traditional, those I have adapted from the recipes learned from family and friends from various cultures, and some I stumbled across while looking for something to do with the vegetables or other foods in the refrigerator when I had not had time to go shopping!

The essence of all of these recipes, however, has come from the foundations of cooking in my culture. The way I was taught to present a meal, the love and care that goes into the preparation of each dish, and the pride taken in providing delicious, nurturing sustenance are lessons learned that I continue to treasure.

The style of cuisine that is encouraged in this book is also a way of eating with which people from around the regions of the Mediterranean are already familiar: having a variety of dishes from which to choose (we never ate just one dish — there were always several to choose from), and an individual approach to cooking in which the quantities of ingredients are adjusted to suit your own taste. In the Middle East and in Europe, variations have occurred in standard recipes for traditional fare as each region or even each family have modified the recipes according to their own likes and dislikes, or even according to the availability of ingredients during any given season.

This brings me to make a point regarding measurements in this book. I was not trained to cook using cup or spoon measurements, even from the beginning. It was always 'handfuls' of this, 'pinches' of that and 'splashes' or 'slurps' of the other. The more you cook, the more you know, see, smell or taste that the quantities are right. I would strongly encourage the cook to vary the quantities of ingredients given — to be creative; to adjust the taste to suit yourself. The measurements given in these recipes, therefore, are to be used as a guide, and a little more or less of anything will not ruin or change a recipe to any great extent. It is all part of getting to know the ingredients yourself. So, relax and enjoy your cooking time. This is the surest recipe of all for a good meal.

Ingredients

There may be a number of ingredients with which you are not familiar. These, however, are easily found in stores or markets these days due to the influence of many different cultures on our cuisine.

Coriander (fresh) Used extensively in Asian and Middle Eastern cuisine, fresh coriander can now be found in many greengrocer shops and supermarkets as well as Asian specialty stores.

Allspice (pimento) This comes in whole or ground form. In the whole form it resembles large peppercorns, but brown rather than black. It is most often found in its ground form and resembles cinnamon. It is not as sweet as cinnamon, and has a slightly hotter flavour. If allspice is unavailable, you could substitute a mixture of equal parts of cinnamon, ground cloves and black pepper.

Pine nuts Now available in many places such as health food shops, Asian and Middle Eastern specialty stores, and even supermarkets. They are actually the seeds from a certain variety of pine cone. Slivered or sliced almonds can be used as a substitute, but have a different flavour to pine nuts.

Tahini This is a paste made from ground sesame seeds. Tahini is available in health food shops, Middle Eastern specialty stores, and, due to expanding popularity, even supermarkets. There is no substitute for tahini in the recipes contained in this book.

Mustard seeds These come in either yellow or dark brown, the dark brown seeds being slightly smaller than the yellow variety. They can often be purchased in bulk form from health food stores or from Indian specialty stores. The yellow seeds are usually used for mustards and pickling, while the brown seeds are used to spice curries and dips.

Burghul This is cracked wheat and can now be bought in health food stores and supermarkets, or in bulk from Middle Eastern specialty stores. Sometimes it is labelled as 'bulgur' or crushed wheat.

Vietnamese mint A very pungent variety of mint which has spear-shaped leaves that are variegated with brown. It has more of an aromatic taste rather than a 'minty' one. It is quite strong, so use it sparingly. There is no real substitute for this flavour.

Tips Before You Start

☐ Always buy food in season.
You have probably heard this said a million times before, but it is worth saying again. Today we can buy most fresh produce at most times of the year, so we tend not to take much notice of seasonal availability. This is fine, and I think in many ways we are lucky to be able to appease our cravings for certain types of fruit and vegetables at almost any time of the year. However, there is no doubt that foods have seasons for fairly good reasons. For example, the flavour of tomatoes at the end of summer confirms that this is exactly the right time for tomatoes. Produce in season is always fresher and more flavoursome.

☐ Be adventurous — do not be afraid to try new combinations.
By experimenting, you can discover flavours that appeal to your own taste. While some herbs and spices do lend themselves to certain vegetables or meats, there are few boundaries that will limit your imagination. Remember, the enjoyment of exploration is the main advice.

☐ Use your hands.
They are one of the most efficient tools in the kitchen. Mix, squeeze, toss — the applications are many and the pleasure great.

☐ A mortar and pestle is another very handy tool for many jobs in the kitchen.

It can be used to crush peppercorns, rock salt, and other herbs and spices; and crushing garlic in this way brings out the pungent flavour more strongly.

☐ Salt brings out the flavour of foods.

We have all heard the warnings about too much salt in our diet, and accepted what our doctors have been saying to us regarding this matter. However, traditional cooks from all over the world still use salt in the preparation of most savoury dishes. There is no denying that it does make a difference to the flavour. My advice, therefore, is to use it according to your own taste (or that of your doctor!). It is more important to remember that processed foods often have a much higher concentration of salt in them than one would sprinkle on freshly prepared foods.

☐ Take some time in the kitchen.

Unfortunately, today's busy lifestyle often leaves us with little time to dawdle through the kitchen cupboards and refrigerator. It is no surprise that the more time you spend thinking about and preparing a meal, the more successful it is bound to be. Most of these recipes are quick and easy, but there are a few which really require some forethought and preparation. Perhaps keeping in mind the amount of time you have will help you decide which of these recipes you might try at any given time.

☐ Take pride in the way you serve your food.

Even if a meal has the most delicious of flavours, it will lose something if its presentation is given no consideration. The choice of bowl or serving dish, the size and shape of a platter, and the combination of colours and the garnishes can make all the difference to the way your meal is received.

☐ Use sharp knives.

Having to saw or hack through vegetables spoils their appearance and texture. Herbs such as parsley respond best to one clean slice, so that the leaves are not bruised and the flavoursome oils are retained to be released in the mouth when chewing.

☐ Have a selection of olive oils and vinegars on hand for different purposes.
More information is contained in *Oils, Vinegars, Dressings and Marinades* (see pages 46-48).

Storage

☐ Fresh herbs such as parsley, coriander, and basil, ie those with softer, more succulent leaves, keep best when wrapped in paper towel, placed in a plastic bag (untied, so that air can get in) and stored in a refrigerator. They will last about a week or 10 days stored in this way, because the moisture from the plastic is absorbed by the paper towel, preventing the herb from becoming wet and slimy. Most vegetables can also be stored using the same principle, such as broccoli, beans, leeks, and capsicums. Mushrooms are best stored in a paper bag, without plastic.

☐ Olive oils are best kept out of direct sunlight. Sometimes buying in bulk and decanting into bottles made of dark glass is more economical, and easier to manage.

☐ Keep potatoes out of sunlight. Place into paper bags, or keep in a cupboard to prolong their life, and discourage sprouting. Never keep potatoes in plastic bags, as they sweat and rot.

☐ To sterilise empty glass jars and bottles for home-made vinegars, oils and preserves, simply boil them in a large saucepan (preferably stainless steel) with two teaspoons of salt. They can then be allowed to cool and dry on their own, or can be placed into a medium to low oven to be heat-dried, until thoroughly dry.

Dips 8

sauces

Universally popular side dishes often come in the form of dips and sauces because of their versatility. You can use some dips as sauces and some sauces as dips.

The following recipes will indicate the ways in which dips and sauces can be used to accent various dishes. Once you have tried some of these recipes as the recommended accompaniments, you will be able to decide how else you could use them. Experiment on your friends and be open to ideas from them. They might offer suggestions on how else these recipes can be used. I have often been told by my friends "This would go really nicely with . . . ". My reply is always "Thanks, I'll try that!". At some stage, so would they.

Front: Seeded Mustard **Top Left:** Eggplant & Yohgurt Dip **Top Right:** Indonesian Onion Sauce

eggplant and yoghurt dip

This is one of the many ways to cook what is probably one of my favourite vegetables. It is often thought that eggplant cannot be cooked without pre-salting it to extract all the bitter juices. In every other case, I do salt eggplant before cooking. However, in this delicious Indian-style recipe, the eggplant is cooked without pre-salting, and I assure you it is far from bitter. It is very refreshing to the palate, and always very popular with my friends.

6 tablespoons vegetable oil
2 teaspoons black mustard seeds
I medium onion, finely chopped
I clove garlic, finely chopped
2 small hot chillies, chopped (optional)
2 medium eggplants, peeled and diced
into squares approximately I cm ($^1/_2$ in)
2 small ripe tomatoes, chopped
2 teaspoons salt
I teaspoon freshly ground black pepper
I teaspoon garam masala
I teaspoon cumin
$^1/_2$ teaspoon turmeric
$^1/_4$ cup (60 ml/2 fl oz)* water or vegetable stock
2 spring onions (shallots), finely chopped
2 tablespoons fresh coriander leaves
I cup (250 ml/8 fl oz) yoghurt

I In a saucepan, place oil and mustard seeds and fry until mustard seeds pop (they crackle as they burst and release their aroma). Add finely chopped onion, garlic and hot chillies (if using) and sauté until onion is transparent.

* Please note: all measurements given are metric, US and imperial units, in that order.

Add eggplant and fry a further 8 minutes, until eggplant softens.

2 Add tomatoes, salt, pepper, garam masala, cumin, turmeric and water or vegetable stock. Allow to simmer for about 5 minutes.

3 Mash with a potato masher or wooden spoon until no large lumps remain. Remove from heat and add spring onions and coriander leaves.

4 Cool until just warm, then add yoghurt and stir well.

Serve with Lebanese bread, melba toast or crusty bread as a dip or with grilled meats, particularly red meat, as a dip or sauce.

houmous (chickpea dip)

For this recipe, it was always my job as a child to grind the chickpeas to a paste once they had been cooked. At first we used a mortar and pestle, and I can remember the 'innovation' of the hand-turned mouli sieve to do the same job. Purists might still like to grind the chickpeas in a mortar and pestle or a sieve, and it does produce a coarser texture which some people prefer. However, an electric blender does cut down on time and aching wrists, especially if you are processing larger quantities.

250 g (8 oz) dried chickpeas
1 litre (32 fl oz/1 ¾ pints) water (to soak chickpeas)
½ teaspoon bicarbonate of soda
1 litre (32 fl oz/1 ¾ pints) water (to cook chickpeas)
2 cloves garlic
1 level teaspoon salt
¼ cup (60 ml/2 fl oz) tahini
juice of 1–1 ½ lemons (according to taste)
1 tablespoon parsley, chopped
sprinkle of cayenne pepper
1 tablespoon extra virgin olive oil

1 Soak chickpeas in water and bicarbonate of soda overnight, so that the chickpeas swell. Drain, wash very well and drain again.

2 Place chickpeas in saucepan with fresh 1 litre (32 fl oz/1³/₄ pints) water and bring to boil. Simmer until chickpeas are soft enough to break or squash between the fingers. Drain, reserving about ¹/₂ cup (125 ml/4 fl oz) of the boiling liquid in case houmous is too thick. Allow chickpeas to cool.

3 Crush garlic and salt in mortar and pestle until a smooth paste is formed. Put crushed garlic, chickpeas and tahini in food processor and process, adding lemon juice to blend. Process until mixture is desired texture. If houmous is too thick, add some of the reserved boiling water during blending.

4 To serve place in a shallow bowl and sprinkle over with chopped parsley and cayenne pepper, and drizzle with extra virgin olive oil.

Serve with Lebanese bread, vegetable crudités, or melba toast as a dip, or with grilled, barbecued or char-grilled meats, lamb and beef in particular, as a dip or sauce.

Cucumber and yoghurt

There are two things in particular to mention about this recipe. Firstly, the type of cucumber you use is quite important in achieving the desired taste. Lebanese cucumbers are smaller than the salad variety normally found in greengrocer shops, and their seeds are minute in comparison. For this reason they are easier to grate and digest, and they are less likely to repeat. A good substitute for Lebanese cucumbers are telegraph cucumbers, which are long and thin, and have the same above-mentioned qualities as the Lebanese variety.

The other thing I wanted to mention here is the use of mint generally, as well as specifically in this recipe. I think that mint is a highly underrated herb. It can be used both fresh and cooked in many dishes to liven up the palate, and in both sweet and savoury foods. The use of mint in this recipe distinguishes it from its Indian cousin, *raita,* and its Greek cousin, *tzatziki,* thereby stamping it as Middle Eastern. If you prefer, you can leave out the mint altogether, but it definitely adds more 'zing' to the flavour.

2–3 medium Lebanese cucumbers
2 level teaspoons salt
2 cloves garlic
2 cups (500 ml/1 pint/16 fl oz) plain yoghurt
¼ cup (15 g/½ oz) fresh mint, chopped

1 Grate cucumbers, leaving the skin on, as this adds colour and texture, and prevents the cucumber repeating. Salt the cucumber with 1 teaspoon of the salt and let stand in colander or strainer for about ½ hour to draw out the moisture.
2 Crush garlic with remaining salt in mortar and pestle. Transfer to a bowl and add yoghurt and mint and mix well.
3 Squeeze all remaining water from cucumber and add the cucumber to the yoghurt. Mix well. Chill.
Serve with meat or vegetable curries as a dip, with char-grilled meats as a dip or sauce, or on top of salads as a dressing.

Optional: Substitute ½ the amount of cucumber with 1 finely chopped, unpeeled green apple. Note: Do not salt the apple with the cucumber, but add it fresh to the yoghurt, just before serving.

a bit on the side

baba ganouj (eggplant dip)

This is a traditional Middle Eastern dish. There are variations of this recipe from different parts of the Mediterranean, some which do not use tahini, but this is one that I like, and it is probably the most well known version. This is one time I prefer to remain purist and mash the cooked eggplant with a pestle, as I prefer a rougher texture, but use a food processor if you like a more even consistency. I also like to roast the eggplants over charcoal because I like the flavour and because it brings back childhood memories. It is good to be a sentimentalist when it comes to the way you prepare certain foods.

2 medium eggplants
2 cloves garlic
I teaspoon salt
$^1/_2$ cup (125 ml/4 fl oz) tahini
juice of I–2 lemons (according to taste)
2 sprigs fresh mint
I tablespoon extra virgin olive oil

I Pierce both whole eggplants with a skewer or fork a few times. Place on a rack and bake in a medium oven until soft (about 30–40 minutes), turning occasionally. Allow to cool.

2 Peel off skin and chop soft flesh. Crush garlic and salt in a mortar and pestle until a smooth paste is formed.

3 In a blender, combine garlic, eggplant flesh and tahini. Blend briefly. Add lemon juice to taste and blend again.

4 To serve place in a shallow platter and garnish with whole fresh mint leaves and drizzle over the extra virgin olive oil.

Serve with Lebanese bread, melba toast or fresh crusty bread as a dip, or with char-grilled meats and kebabs as a dip or sauce.

Opposite: Baba Ganouj

Indonesian Onion Sauce

An Indonesian friend first introduced me to this recipe many years ago. The most vivid memory I have of the first time I tasted it was the fire it lit inside my head and oesophagus. Needless to say, I have since adjusted the amount of chilli to suit my own tolerance level. I suggest you do the same.

2 large brown onions, finely diced
2 cloves garlic, chopped
2–4 fresh hot chillies, chopped or sliced (optional)
2 tablespoons peanut or vegetable oil
$^1/_2$ red capsicum, finely chopped
2 sprigs fresh coriander, chopped
1 teaspoon brown sugar
$^1/_4$ cup (60 ml/2 fl oz) soy sauce
2 teaspoons tomato paste
juice of $^1/_2$ lime
2 teaspoons roasted peanuts, chopped

1 Sauté onion, garlic and chilli in oil until onion is transparent. Add capsicum and sauté for a further 2–3 minutes, so that capsicums are still fairly firm.

2 Add coriander leaves, brown sugar, soy sauce, tomato paste and lime juice. Simmer until sauce thickens (about 10 minutes).

3 To serve place in a bowl and sprinkle with roasted peanuts. Sauce may be served either hot or cold.

Serve with barbecued or roasted meats, or with fish, tofu (either fried or steamed), or steamed vegetables.

a bit on the side

tahini and garlic sauce

This is a favourite of mine because, as well as being delicious, it is so versatile. The flavours complement most meats and vegetables. It goes particularly well with fried fish — a sort of Middle Eastern tartare sauce, only better!

1 clove garlic
1 teaspoon salt
1 ½ cups (375 ml/12 fl oz) tahini
juice of 1–2 lemons (according to taste)
½ cup (125 ml/4 fl oz) cold water
½ teaspoon paprika, either hot or sweet (according to taste)
½ cup (30 g/1 oz) continental (flat leaf) parsley, chopped

1 Crush garlic and salt in mortar and pestle. Transfer to a bowl and mix in tahini.

2 Add lemon juice and enough water to stop the tahini and lemon juice from sticking together in a thick mass. Desired consistency is about that of mayonnaise. Stir in paprika and parsley.

Serve with meats and fish as a sauce, or on top of salads as a dressing. It is excellent as a dressing on sliced ripe tomatoes.

a bit on the side

Seeded mustard with fresh herbs

Although making your own mustard seems time consuming and unnecessary, given that there are so many varieties available, I can assure you that once you have tried this mustard, you will find it hard to go back to the prepared varieties.

15 g (1/2 oz) whole black peppercorns
130 g (41/2 oz) mustard seeds
2/3 cup (155 ml/5 fl oz) white wine vinegar
1/2 cup (125 ml/4 fl oz) dry white wine
3/4 cup (185 ml/6 fl oz) oil, either olive or vegetable oil
2 teaspoons salt
1/2 teaspoon sugar
1 level teaspoon turmeric
1/2 cup (30 g/1 oz) fresh herbs (a mixture of rosemary, thyme and tarragon, or any other herbs of your choice)

1 Combine all ingredients (except herbs), mix, cover, and allow to stand overnight to soften mustard seeds and peppercorns. Place in food processor and process about 3–5 minutes to desired texture or until mixture thickens.

2 Add fresh herbs and blend for a further 1 minute or until all ingredients are well combined.

Makes about 2 cups (500 ml/1 pint/16 fl oz) of mustard, which can be stored in a jar in the refrigerator for up to 3 months.

Serve with roasted, boiled or corned meats, or add to vinegar and oil dressings for salads or to sauces and marinades.

Opposite: Tahini and Garlic Sauce and Toum

toum (garlic paste)

This paste is not for the faint of heart, but if you love garlic as I do, this stuff can become quite addictive. I try to have this paste when I do not have to socialise for at least 24 hours, otherwise I feed it to all the people with whom I am going to socialise within the next 24 hours, so that nobody can complain!

8 cloves garlic, peeled
1 1/2 level teaspoons salt
olive oil (approximately 1 cup [250 ml/8 fl oz])
juice of 1/2 lemon

1 Crush garlic and salt with a mortar and pestle. If your mortar and pestle are small, crush the garlic with the pestle in a bowl. When a smooth paste has formed, add about 1 tablespoonful of oil and mix carefully with pestle until all the oil is absorbed into the paste. Repeat this, adding only enough oil at any one time to be easily mixed in and absorbed into the paste. The paste will swell in volume and take on a slightly yellow colour from the oil. Eventually the paste will begin to ball together in the same way as bread dough balls together. This whole process can also be done in a food processor, gradually pouring in oil through the top of the processor.

2 When the paste reaches this stage, it has absorbed as much oil as it can. The oil takes the sharpness and 'heat' out of the garlic. Stir in the lemon juice. Garlic paste should now have the consistency of mayonnaise.

Use as a marinade for chicken, before barbecuing, grilling or baking. Toum is excellent with meats, fish, chicken and steamed vegetables. This recipe can also be used to make garlic bread by adding a little chopped parsley to the paste before spreading it onto the bread.

home-made yoghurt

If you like to have on hand a reasonable amount of fresh plain yoghurt, it is worthwhile making your own and keeping it in the refrigerator to use in whatever way you like. My mother used to make litres of yoghurt as well as cream cheese and dried yoghurt balls rolled in herbs from the same batch.

Home-made fresh yoghurt is easy to make, and is delicious on its own, if you are a yoghurt fan as I am, or as a tangy addition to many mains. As a child I was always the one to have the first taste of the creamy part of the curd which sets at the top of the yoghurt. I must admit that, as an adult, I will still elbow aside any competition for this most prized part.

This yoghurt keeps in the refrigerator for at least a week.

2 litres (2 quarts/3¼ pints) whole milk
½ cup (125 ml/4 fl oz) plain yoghurt

1 Heat the milk in an enamel or stainless steel saucepan (do not use aluminium) until it reaches boiling point, but do not allow the milk to actually boil. Leave the milk to cool until it is just warm. The test for the correct temperature of the milk is rather unusual, but it is one that has been used traditionally and successfully for years without the use of thermometers. Test by putting your little finger into the warm milk. If you can just tolerate the temperature of the milk up to the count of 40, it has cooled down to the correct temperature to add the culture that is contained in the prepared yoghurt. Stir in the yoghurt gently.

2 Cover with a tight-fitting lid and wrap the whole saucepan in a couple of blankets and place in a warm, dark place for about 12 hours undisturbed.

3 When the yoghurt has set, place in refrigerator and use as desired.

Serve with fresh fruit, grilled meats, spiced rice dishes, curries, or use in salad dressings.

Vegetables
salads
&

rice

These things do not have to be boring. Be imaginative, take risks and you will be surprised at the results you can achieve. While many of these dishes are presented, for the purposes of this book, as the 'bit on the side', they can also be served as entrées, antipasto, or main meals, if that is your fancy.

The main point here, however, is to demonstrate that vegetables and rice need not be plain to accompany the traditional 'main' part of the meal. There is a place for plain steamed vegetables and rice, but I have never been able to help myself in creating more interesting alternatives.

Antipasta: Roasted Banana Chillies, Roasted Capsicum, Marinated Zucchinis and Dried Tomatoes

Spicy green beans

Surprisingly, the richness of the sauce in this dish does not detract from the flavour of the beans but rather, enhances it. There is also the option of cooking the beans slightly longer in the sauce if you prefer your vegetables a little softer. Taste them during the cooking time to determine the right texture for you.

I large onion, sliced
2 cloves garlic, chopped
4 tablespoons olive oil
2 tablespoons parsley, chopped
2 tablespoons fresh coriander, chopped
I small hot chilli, chopped (optional)
$\frac{1}{2}$ kg (I lb) green beans or snake beans, stringed
and cut into 5 cm (2 in) lengths
salt and black pepper, to taste
I teaspoon ground allspice (pimento)
2 medium ripe tomatoes, skinned and chopped

I Brown the onion and garlic in oil, then add parsley, coriander and chilli. Stir well and cook a further 2 minutes.

2 Add beans, salt, pepper and allspice and stir over heat for about 2–3 minutes. Add tomatoes.

3 Cover and simmer, stirring occasionally. The tomatoes should reduce down to quite a thick sauce.

Serve with any meats, either cold or hot, or potatoes, cooked any way, or as a stew-style dish with rice.

a bit on the side

Spicy potatoes

Potatoes are delicious vegetables and can be prepared in many ways. Often when there is not much else in the house, I serve this dish as a main meal with a leafy green salad. It is very satisfying, nutritious and yummy. I once surprised a couple of friends by walking into the kitchen, as they remember, "with a brown paper bag full of potatoes, and walking out a short time later with a meal for 4 people." Magic!

I large onion, finely sliced
$1/4$ cup (60 ml/2 fl oz) olive oil
I small hot chilli, chopped (optional)
2 tablespoons parsley, chopped
I kg (2 lbs) old potatoes, peeled, diced and parboiled
salt and black pepper, to taste
I teaspoon allspice (pimento)

1 Brown onion in olive oil. Add chilli and parsley. Cook for a further 2 minutes.

2 Add potatoes, salt, pepper and allspice and stir together well. Cover and cook on low heat for about 15 minutes or until potatoes are soft, stirring occasionally.

Serve with meat curries, or grilled meats, either hot or cold, or with leafy green salads.

garlic and lemon snake beans

If snake beans are hard for you to obtain, you can always substitute green string beans. There is a difference in flavour and texture however. Snake beans are easy to grow and very prolific. They are climbing beans, and I have seen them grown very successfully in pots on a sunny balcony.

This is the way these beans were traditionally prepared in my home.

½ kg (1 lb) snake beans
2 cloves garlic
½–1 teaspoon salt
1 ½ tablespoons extra virgin olive oil
juice of ½ lemon

1 Cut beans into lengths of approximately 6 cm (2½ in), and steam them.
2 Crush garlic and salt into a smooth paste in a bowl. Add beans to garlic while they are still warm. Pour over the olive oil and toss the beans to coat. Add lemon juice and toss again.
Serve with grilled meats, potato dishes, or anything you want to add a 'tang' to.

Opposite: Garlic and Lemon Snake Beans and Spicy Potatoes

beetroot salad

The flavour of caraway is a delicious combination with fresh beetroot, and the colour of the beetroot itself adds flair to any plate. If the beetroots are quite small, you can actually leave them whole instead of dicing them.

4 medium, raw beetroots
I clove garlic, finely chopped
I teaspoon caraway seeds
salt, to taste
freshly ground black pepper, to taste
2 tablespoons extra virgin olive oil
I tablespoon apple cider vinegar

I Remove leaves from beetroots, leaving about 6 cm (2$^{1}/_{2}$ in) of the stems still attached. Boil beetroots in their skins until cooked, about 20 minutes. Test with a skewer.

2 Allow to cool then remove skins. Dice beetroot into bite-sized pieces and place into a bowl. Add chopped garlic, caraway seeds, salt, pepper, oil and vinegar and toss together.

3 Allow to stand for about $^{1}/_{2}$ hour before serving to allow the caraway seeds to soften and release their flavour into the beetroot.

Serve with any meat, fish or poultry dishes, especially barbecued meats, or with potato, rice or pasta dishes.

Oregano and onion salad

When I first served this salad to some friends they were astounded that a salad could be made from herbs alone. It was an instant hit, and lamb kebabs can never again be served in my house without this unusual and particularly tangy salad accompanying them. One friend in particular says that "only an Arab would eat herbs in this way". This Arab in particular!

I cup (60 g/2 oz) fresh oregano, leaves only
I small white or red (Spanish) onion, finely diced
$^1/_4$ teaspoon salt
2 tablespoons extra virgin olive oil
I–2 tablespoons lemon juice

I Strip oregano leaves from stalks and place into a bowl. Add finely diced onion. Sprinkle with salt and rub the salt gently into the diced onion with the tips of your fingers. This helps the flavour of the onion to disperse through the dressing, and helps stop the onion from repeating.

2 Drizzle over the olive oil and toss through the salad. Add lemon juice and toss again.

Serve with char-grilled meats, or kebabs (particularly lamb), or with lentil dishes or potato dishes.

roasted capsicum

I have suggested in this recipe that you use mixed coloured capsicums, because it adds more visual interest to the dish. It can, of course, be made using capsicums of one colour, but red coloured capsicums have a different flavour from the green and the yellow varieties. It is really up to your individual taste again on this occasion.

The capsicums can also be roasted over the grill section of a coal barbecue for an added 'smoky' flavour.

4 medium capsicums (mixed colours)
I clove garlic, finely chopped
salt and black pepper, to taste
I tablespoon extra virgin olive oil
2 teaspoons balsamic vinegar

I Place whole washed capsicums on roasting rack and bake in medium to high oven, turning until skin becomes slightly scorched on all sides. Remove from grill and place in a bowl. Cover with a tea towel for about 20 minutes, to keep in the steam and loosen the skin. The capsicums will be soft.
2 Peel, then remove stem and seeds. Slice into strips and place in a bowl.
3 Add finely chopped garlic, salt, pepper, olive oil and vinegar. Allow to marinate for about I hour before serving. The marinated capsicums can also be kept covered in the refrigerator for up to I week.
Serve with cheeses, cold meats, pasta, or on sandwiches, in green salads and with all varieties of grilled or barbecued meats.

roasted banana chillies

Similar to roasted capsicum, these banana chillies are very attractive served whole with the stalk still attached. They are not hot. While they are called chillies, banana chillies are more like capsicum in their 'sweetness' of flavour.

6 red banana chillies
2 cloves garlic, finely chopped
salt and freshly ground black pepper, to taste
1 ½ tablespoons extra virgin olive oil
1 tablespoon balsamic or red wine vinegar
few sprigs parsley, to garnish

1 Grill banana chillies, turning until slightly charred or scorched on all sides. Avoid grilling stalks. Put on a plate and cover for about 20 minutes with a tea towel to keep in the steam and loosen skins.

2 Peel off skin, but leave chillies whole. Arrange on a platter and sprinkle on garlic, salt and pepper, and drizzle over olive oil. Add vinegar last. Decorate with a few sprigs of parsley.

Serve with grilled meats, cheeses, salads, or potato dishes.

leeks vinaigrette

The first time I saw a leek used as a vegetable on its own, I was taken with the look of it as well as with its flavour. I now grow my own leeks so that I can have smaller ones to cook whole, as well as large ones to use in soups. The younger, more tender leeks suit this style of preparation.

4 medium leeks, trimmed and washed
10 whole black peppercorns
I bay leaf
$^1/_2$ cup (125 ml/4 fl oz) dry white wine
I cup (250 ml/8 fl oz) water
2 slices of lemon
I clove garlic, finely chopped
salt, to taste
freshly ground black pepper, to taste
2 tablespoons extra virgin olive oil
1-2 tablespoons white wine vinegar
I teaspoon fresh parsley, chopped

1 Trim leeks, leaving approximately 6 cm (2$^1/_2$ in) of the greens on the end of the white part. Wash very well to remove all the dirt.
2 Place in a shallow pan with the whole peppercorns, bay leaf, white wine, water and lemon, and poach for 10–15 minutes. Test them for tenderness with a skewer. When cooked, drain and place onto a serving platter.
3 Sprinkle over garlic, salt, freshly ground black pepper, olive oil and vinegar, and garnish with chopped parsley.
Serve hot or cold with any type of meat, fish or poultry, or potato dishes, or with cheeses and fresh crusty bread.

Opposite: Beetroot Salad, Tomato, Onion and Coriander Salad and Leeks Vinaigrette

a bit on the side

dried tomatoes

Sun-dried tomatoes are a very popular addition to the pantry these days. Originally they were a way of preserving tomatoes for use throughout the winter months. To dry tomatoes in the sun is impractical where I live, but the same 'dried' result can be achieved by drying them in your oven.

1 kg (2 lbs) Italian plum tomatoes, firm and ripe
salt
black pepper
8 whole garlic cloves
10–12 sprigs of fresh oregano or basil
2–4 bay leaves
dried chillies (optional)
olive oil (enough to fill the jar in which you pack the tomatoes)

1 Cut the tomatoes in half lengthways and place them (cut side up) on a baking rack over a baking dish. Sprinkle with the salt and pepper as desired. Sit the whole garlic cloves on top of the cut tomatoes, spaced around as desired. Lay the sprigs of oregano or basil on top of the tomatoes.

2 Place tomatoes into a very low oven with the door held ajar with a wooden spoon. They will take 9–12 hours to dry, depending on their size. Check them as you reach the 9 hour mark, and then approximately hourly after that. They should be dried, but still plump to the touch. Do not let them become crispy, as they will not reconstitute in the oil.

3 When sufficiently dried, allow to cool completely. Pack the tomatoes, herbs, roasted garlic cloves, bay leaves and chillies (if desired), into a clean, sterilised jar. Fill the jar with olive oil until all the tomatoes are covered.

4 Tomatoes will be ready in 4–7 days, and will keep for up to 1 year.

Serve with cold meats, cheeses, or plain crispy bread, or in pasta dishes and salads, on pizzas or sandwiches, or as part of an antipasto platter.

tomato, Onion and coriander salad

This quick and easy salad leaves a lovely fresh taste in the mouth. I often need to make double the quantity, because I have found it to be very popular with friends, and I always know I will want some for lunch the next day!

This salad keeps overnight in the refrigerator.

¹/₂ cup (30 g/1 oz) fresh coriander, chopped
2–3 medium, firm, ripe tomatoes, finely diced
1 medium red (Spanish) onion, finely diced
1-2 tablespoons cider vinegar
2 teaspoons extra virgin olive oil
1 level teaspoon salt
¹/₂ teaspoon freshly ground black pepper

1 Mix all ingredients together. Serve salad slightly chilled.
Serve with grilled meats or fish, or with curries or egg dishes.

tabbouli (parsley salad)

I know there are many recipes around for this traditional and delicious Middle Eastern parsley salad, and I know everybody remembers their Mum's cooking as being the best. Well, this is my Mum's way of making tabbouli, and I, too, say it is the best!

¼ cup (45 g/1½ oz) burghul (cracked wheat)
3 cups (185 g/6 oz) fresh continental
(flat leaf) parsley, finely chopped
⅔ cup (37 g/1¼ oz) fresh mint, chopped
1 small onion, finely diced or 5 spring onions (shallots),
including greens, finely chopped
2 level teaspoons salt
¼ teaspoon finely ground black pepper
1 teaspoon ground allspice (pimento)
2 large ripe tomatoes, finely diced
¼ cup (60 ml/2 fl oz) extra virgin olive oil
juice of ½–1 lemon (according to taste)

1 Soak the burghul in cold water for 10 minutes. Drain well.

2 In a bowl mix burghul, parsley and mint. Add chopped onions, and sprinkle over the salt, pepper and allspice. Rub the spices gently into the onion to help disperse the flavours and to help prevent the onion from repeating.

3 Add the tomatoes, olive oil and lemon juice and toss together. Chill for about 10–15 minutes.

To serve place in lettuce cups, and serve with grilled or fried meat or chicken, or with potato dishes or egg dishes.

marinated zucchinis

The longer these are left to marinate, the more the zucchinis absorb the flavours of the dressing. Arrange them overlapping in an attractive dish so that they can be served straight at the table when they are ready. If you like chillies, you can finely chop one or two and sprinkle them over the top during the marinating process, to add bite and a little contrast in colour.

8–10 zucchinis (dark green or yellow, or both)
2 teaspoons salt
3–4 tablespoons olive oil
$1/4$ cup (15 g/$1/2$ oz) fresh mint, chopped
1 teaspoon freshly ground black pepper
2 medium cloves garlic, chopped
$1/4$ cup (60 ml/2 fl oz) red wine vinegar

1 Trim the zucchinis and slice them lengthways into slices about $1/2$ cm ($1/4$ in) thick. Sprinkle with salt and allow them to stand in a colander or strainer for about 1 hour. Pat the slices dry.

2 Shallow fry the zucchini slices in the olive oil until they just begin to turn golden. Remove them and arrange the slices in a shallow serving dish. Sprinkle the chopped mint and black pepper over the zucchinis.

3 Add the chopped garlic to the remaining oil and sauté lightly until just transparent. Add the red wine vinegar and allow the mixture to simmer for about 3–5 minutes, until the acidic taste of the vinegar dissipates slightly. Pour the warm vinegar and oil mixture over the zucchinis.

4 Allow them to cool and marinate for about 4 hours before serving. The zucchinis can be served at room temperature or chilled.

Serve with any char-grilled, barbecued or roasted meats, or with potato dishes or egg dishes.

a bit on the side

Chickpea salad

An unusual salad, but if you like chickpeas, this is an easy and tasty dish. In my household, we sometimes used to have this dish at breakfast time, served with a drizzle of tahini over the top.

Breakfast foods from different cultures can seem quite unconventional, even unthinkable, to people outside that culture, so if you are not game to try this one for breakfast (served warm), then try it at lunchtime or dinnertime, but do try it.

250 g (8 oz) dried chickpeas
I litre (32 fl oz/1 ^{3}/$_4$ pints) cold water (to soak chickpeas)
^{1}/$_2$ teaspoon bicarbonate of soda
I litre (32 fl oz/1 ^{3}/$_4$ pints) cold water (to cook chickpeas)
I large clove garlic
I teaspoon salt
^{1}/$_2$ cup (30 g/1 oz) continental (flat leaf) parsley, chopped
^{1}/$_4$ cup (60 ml/2 fl oz) extra virgin olive oil
juice of I lemon

I Soak chickpeas in water and bicarbonate of soda overnight so that they swell. Drain and then wash the chickpeas thoroughly.

2 Drain again and place chickpeas in a saucepan with the litre (32 fl oz/ 1 ^{3}/$_4$ pints) of fresh water and bring them to the boil. Simmer until chickpeas are soft enough to squash between the thumb and forefinger. Remove any scum from the water that appears during the cooking process.

3 Crush the garlic and salt in a bowl with a pestle. Add the drained chickpeas, parsley, oil and lemon juice and toss together well. This salad can be served warm or cold.

Serve with all char-grilled or barbecued meats, especially red meats.

Opposite: Pilau with Pine Nuts and Raisins

a bit on the side

pilau with pine nuts and raisins

A Bangladeshi friend of mine once told me that the "beauty" of the rice dish accompanying spicy curries was a very important aspect of the meal, because it was served as a centrepiece for the table and therefore its own decorative effect indicated the sumptuousness of what was to be served with it.

This rice dish makes a great centrepiece when served piled high on a beautiful shallow platter. Its mixture of spicy, savoury and sweet never fails to attract comment.

3 cups (475 g/15 oz) long grain white rice or basmati rice
70 g (2 ^{1}/$_2$ oz) unsalted butter
^{1}/$_4$ cup (30 g/1 oz) pine nuts
^{1}/$_4$ cup (30 g/1 oz) raisins
6 whole cloves
1 x 3 cm (1 ^{1}/$_4$ in) piece cinnamon bark
^{1}/$_2$ teaspoon salt
^{1}/$_2$ teaspoon finely ground black pepper
1 teaspoon turmeric
cold water
^{1}/$_4$ cup (15 g/^{1}/$_2$ oz) whole fresh coriander leaves
1 small red chilli, sliced (optional)

1 Wash rice and drain well. Melt the butter in a saucepan and add the pine nuts. Stir constantly until they turn a golden brown colour. Remove from the heat and add the raisins, cloves and cinnamon bark and stir until they are all coated with the butter.
2 Return to the heat, add the rice, salt, pepper and turmeric and stir about another ^{1}/$_2$ minute or more to coat the rice with the butter.

3 Pour over enough cold water to cover the level of the rice by about 2 cm (³/₄ in). Stir. Bring the water to the boil, then reduce the heat to a simmer, cover the saucepan with a tight-fitting lid and allow to cook until all the water has been absorbed and the rice is cooked through.

4 Allow to stand in the covered saucepan for 5–10 minutes so the rice will become fluffy. Pile the pilau onto a platter and sprinkle over the whole coriander leaves and slices of chilli.

Serve with curries, stews, char-grilled meats, satays, or fish.

Pickles

chutneys

This section contains a mixture of pickles and chutneys ranging from the comparatively ordinary to the more bizarre, although it depends on your perspective as to which of these you think are which. I myself used to find choko pickles most bizarre!

The beauty of pickles and chutneys is that they can be stored for long periods of time, and they can be used to 'dress up' anything from leftovers to gourmet curries. Here are a few suggestions for you to try.

Platter: Stuffed Pickled Baby Eggplants, Marinated Olives and Home-made Preserved Olives

Choko pickles

Everybody with a choko vine needs at least one choko recipe.

1 kg (2 lbs) chokos
$^1/_2$ kg (1 lb) brown onions
$^1/_3$ cup (90 g/3 oz) salt
cold water
750 ml (24 fl oz) brown malt vinegar
750 g (1$^1/_2$ lbs) brown sugar
2 teaspoons mustard seeds
2 teaspoons fresh ginger, grated
2 teaspoons turmeric
2 teaspoons dry mustard
2 teaspoons curry powder
$^3/_4$ cup (90 g/3 oz) plain white flour

1 Peel and dice chokos and onions into $^1/_2$ cm ($^1/_4$ in) cubes. Sprinkle over the salt, toss, then cover with cold water and let stand overnight.

2 Next day, drain and rinse the chokos and onions. Place about 600 ml (20 fl oz/1 pint) of vinegar with sugar, mustard seeds and ginger into a stainless steel or enamel saucepan. Boil for 3–5 minutes. Add the chokos and onions and bring the mixture back to the boil for approximately 5 minutes.

3 Mix the dry ingredients into a smooth paste with the remaining 150 ml (5 fl oz) of vinegar. Remove the saucepan from the heat and add the paste to the mixture, then stir well while off the heat. Return to a simmer for about another 10–15 minutes until the pickles thicken.

4 Pour into hot sterilised jars, allow to cool, then seal.

Serve with any cold or smoked meats, particularly red meats, or hard yellow cheeses, or with grilled or barbecued sausages.

Stuffed pickled baby eggplants

These are rather unusual, and a little time consuming, but worth the effort, especially if you like pickled things generally. A word of warning, though: try not to kiss anybody who is easily offended after eating one of these, as the garlic matures during the pickling time.

12–14 plump baby eggplants, approximately 5–6 cm
(2–2$^{1}/_{2}$ in) long and 2–3 cm ($^{3}/_{4}$–1$^{1}/_{4}$ in) in diameter
cold water
3–4 cloves garlic
2 teaspoons salt
2 small hot chillies (optional)
$^{1}/_{2}$ red capsicum
75 g (2$^{1}/_{2}$ oz) shelled walnuts, crushed coarsely
olive oil, enough to fill jar in which you preserve the eggplants

1 Remove the stalk and top from the eggplants. Slit them lengthways with the pointy end of a small knife, starting 1 cm ($^{1}/_{2}$ in) from the top and finishing 1 cm ($^{1}/_{2}$ in) from the bottom end of each eggplant.

2 Place the eggplants in a saucepan with enough cold water to cover them, then bring the water to the boil and allow the eggplants to cook for approximately 8 minutes, until they are firm, but spongy to touch. The colour will change to a dark grey. Drain them very well and allow to dry thoroughly.

3 To make stuffing, process the garlic, salt, hot chillies and capsicum in a food processor. Place this mixture into a bowl, and mix in the crushed walnuts.

4 Stuff portions of the mixture into each eggplant until they are quite full. Pack the stuffed eggplants into a jar. Cover with a piece of fine mesh,

a bit on the side

a strainer, or even chicken wire — anything that will allow the moisture to drain away as the salt extracts any bitter juices from the eggplants. Invert the jar over a cup or bowl which just fits the rim of the jar. Allow to stand for at least 24 hours, or until there is no more evidence of the juices draining off. Turn the jar upright and fill with enough olive oil to cover the eggplants.

5 Leave these to pickle for at least I week before using. They will last up to 6 months in a cupboard if the eggplants are kept covered with oil.

Serve with egg dishes, potato dishes, and all meats, either grilled or barbecued, or with hard cheeses and fresh crusty bread.

mint and coriander chUtney

Adjust the ratios of garlic, coriander and mint in this recipe to create your own designer chutney!

3 cloves garlic
I 1/2 teaspoons salt
3 cups (185 g/6 oz) of herbs (mixed mints such as peppermint, spearmint, and common mint, with coriander [leaves only])
1/4 cup (15 g/1/2 oz) Vietnamese mint (optional)
1/2 cup (125 ml/4 fl oz) white wine vinegar
I tablespoon extra virgin olive oil

I Process garlic and salt until the garlic is fairly fine. Add the herbs and mint and blend until fine, adding a little vinegar to keep the mixture moving.

2 Add the oil and process again to blend the oil in well.

3 Place in a cool, sterilised jar, and use as desired.

Serve with meats, fish, curries and potato dishes.

Opposite: Mint and Coriander Chutney and Pickled Vegetables

a bit on the side

home-made preserved olives

Splitting the flesh of fresh green olives allows the bitter juices to be extracted and the pickling juices to be absorbed. The longer the olives marinate the less bitter they will be.

1 kg (2 lbs) fresh green olives
$1/4$ cup (60 g/2 oz) salt
1 cup (250 ml/8 fl oz) olive oil
$1/4$ cup (60 ml/2 fl oz) vinegar
several whole sprigs of herbs such as rosemary, thyme, oregano, dill, and fennel (either one or a mixture of several of these)
1 or 2 fresh hot chillies (optional)
2 slices of lemon, cut into quarters
1 cup (250 ml/8 fl oz) warm water, or enough to cover the olives once they are packed into jars

1 Split each olive with a paring knife in 3 or 4 places, or hit with a pestle to split the flesh of the olive. Place the olives into a bowl and sprinkle over the salt, olive oil, vinegar, herbs, chillies and lemon.

2 Place in the jars and allow to stand overnight. The next day, fill the jars with the warm water. Adding the water the next day allows the olives to absorb the salt and oil, so that the flesh of the olives stays firmer. The olives can tend to deteriorate more quickly if the water is added at the same time as the oil, because they absorb the water first, rather than the oil.

3 Leave to stand for at least 2 weeks before eating.

Serve with any cheeses or fresh crusty bread, salads, egg dishes, potato dishes, or pasta dishes.

Marinated olives

It is often too time consuming or inconvenient to make one's own olives from scratch, so marinating olives which have already been preserved in brine (bought from any delicatessen or supermarket), is another way of having a delicious accompaniment on hand at any time. Apart from the taste, I always find the addition of herbs and spices to black olives a very attractive alternative. The colours of the seeds, herbs and red chillies visually spices up any table.

½ kg (1 lb) black olives preserved in brine
(kalamata olives or any other fleshy, plump, black variety)
½ teaspoon fennel seeds
½ teaspoon caraway seeds
1 teaspoon dried oregano
1 red chilli, chopped (optional)
3 teaspoons fresh parsley, chopped
1 tablespoon extra virgin olive oil
1–2 cloves garlic, chopped
1 bay leaf
3 teaspoons cider vinegar
½ teaspoon whole black peppercorns

1 Mix all the ingredients together in a bowl. Fill jars and seal.
2 Allow to stand for about 1 week so that all the flavours permeate, and the seeds soften. Serve as desired.
Serve with cheeses and crusty white bread, or with salads, egg dishes, potato dishes or pasta dishes.

Pickled Vegetables

Rarely have I looked into the pantry of a Mediterranean or Asian household and not seen jars and jars of pickled and preserved goodies. They are a favourite accompaniment in many cultures. In my family household, it was sometimes a problem deciding which pickled thing we would eat at any given time. My mother always had on hand different pickles to please all of our varied tastes. The hard thing for me was that I liked them all, so I had to be careful of 'pickle overdose'!

This is the basic recipe for pickling liquid that will suit quite a variety of vegetables. The quantities suggested are suitable for enough vegetables to fill a 2 to $2^1/_2$ litre (2 quarts/$3^1/_4$ pints to $2^1/_2$ quarts/4 pints) jar. I would suggest that you taste the pickling liquid before filling the jar, and adjust the flavours to suit yourself. I know from my own family's tastes that some people prefer sweet pickles and some prefer salty. Likewise adjust the vinegar to water ratio to suit yourself.

You may like to colour the more colourless vegetables, such as cauliflower, white turnips, fennel bulbs or cabbage, by slicing a small raw beetroot and placing the slices on top of your pickling vegetables before you pour the pickling liquid over them.

Other vegetables, besides those already mentioned, that are suitable for pickling are green tomatoes, carrots, chillies, capsicums and gherkin cucumbers, or a mixture of several of these. The method is always the same.

Always choose firm, unblemished vegetables for pickling.

1 ¹/₂–2 kg (3 lbs–4lbs) vegetables
(depending on the vegetables you choose)
few sprigs of fresh herbs of choice
1 cup (225 g/7 oz) sugar
1 cup (225 g/7 oz) salt
2 cups (500 ml/1 pint/16 fl oz) white wine vinegar
3–4 cups (750 ml/24 fl oz–1 litre/32 fl oz/1³/₄ pints) cold water

1 Wash the vegetables in cold water. Slice or cut the vegetables as desired. Pack the jar with the vegetables and herbs.

2 In a stainless steel or enamel saucepan, bring the sugar, salt and vinegar to the boil. Allow the liquid to cool, add the cold water, stir and taste. Adjust amounts of sugar, salt and vinegar if necessary.

3 Pour the liquid over the vegetables, topping up with cold water or vinegar according to taste if the liquid does not cover the vegetables. Seal the jar. Let stand for about 1–2 weeks before using.

Serve with stews, pasta dishes, potato dishes, egg dishes, or with any meat or vegetable dishes.

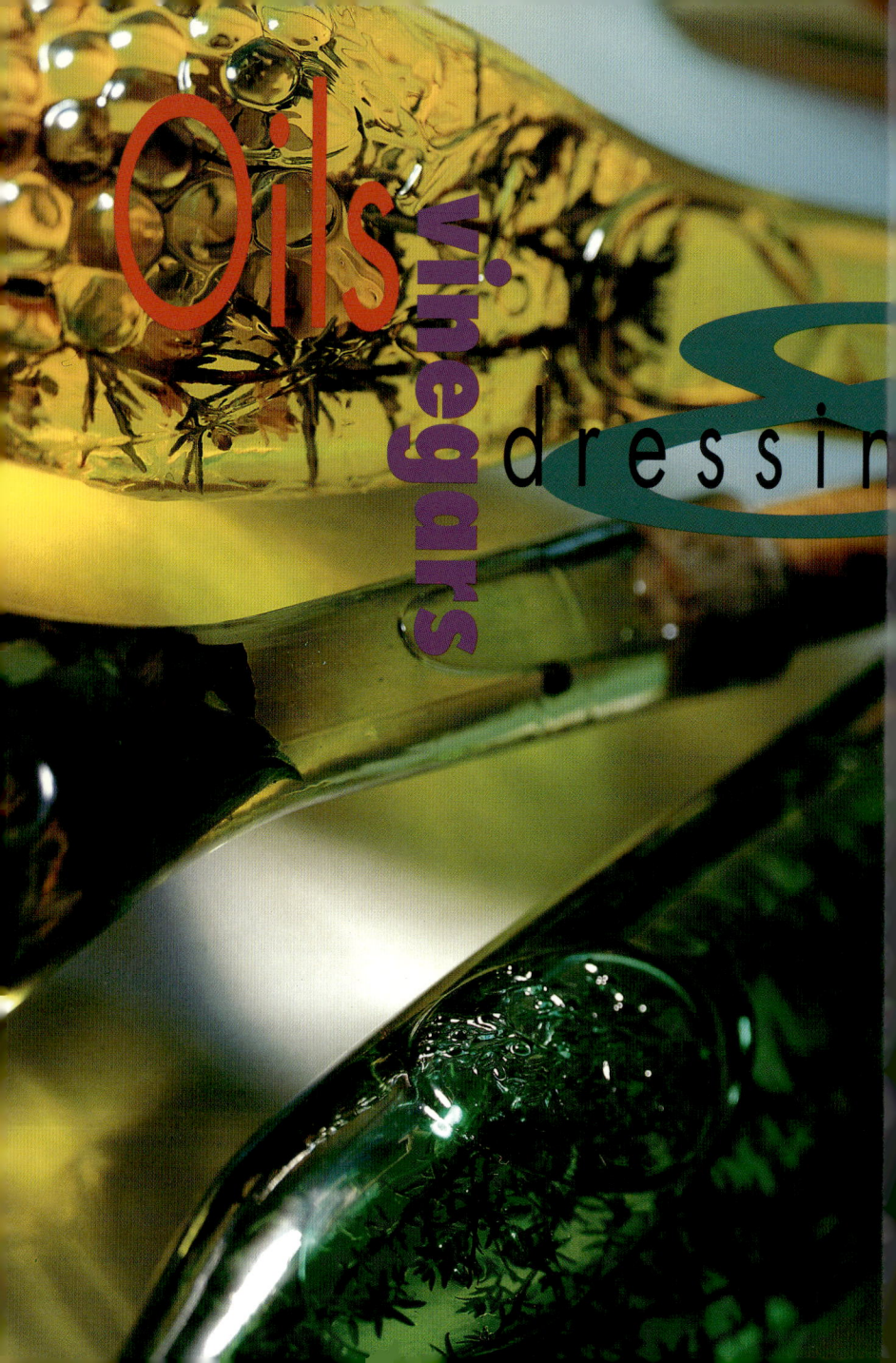

Oils
vinegars
dressin

marinades

There are many different types of oils available for use in cooking and salads these days. Olive oils are the main focus in this book, because they are my favourite and they are the ones which were always used in my home. Middle Eastern and Mediterranean people have traditionally used olive oils as olives were and still are a major crop in those regions. For similar reasons, other types of oils, for example peanut oil, are used in other cuisines. While peanut and other oils are used in one or two of the recipes in this book, the use of olive oil definitely predominates. In recent times, the healthy properties of olive oil have become more known, so this is a good reason to use olive oil if you do not use it already.

Opposite: Herb Vinegars and Oils

Olive oils range in quality from pomace to extra light, light, pure (a standard olive oil), virgin and extra virgin. They also range in flavour depending on their country of origin. Varieties include Spanish, Italian, Greek, Lebanese, Portuguese, French and Australian. Due to the variation in flavours, I prefer to keep a range on hand to suit my needs, and moods, at any time. It is difficult to describe in words the variations in flavour, but I will suggest a broader rule of thumb for their use as far as quality goes.

☐ Extra Virgin or Virgin Olive Oil — Always use this for salads and raw foods because it is the richest in flavour and colour — cold pressed is best! Do not be concerned about sediment in the bottle, as this indicates the oil's purity. If you cannot obtain extra virgin or virgin oil, use pure olive oil.

☐ Pure Olive Oil — Use mainly for shallow frying or sautéeing. Extra virgin or virgin olive oil can be substituted if a richer flavour is desired.

☐ Light or Extra Light Olive Oil — Best for deep frying, as they have a more subtle flavour. Light olive oils allow foods to retain their own taste and give a light crispiness to batters.

☐ Pomace Olive Oil — Pronounced pomaché, this is made from the final pressing of olives. I rarely use this oil, but it can be used for frying.

As with oils, there are many varieties of vinegars from which to choose, and it is true that some are more suitable than others for specific purposes. There are few hard and fast rules and it is only by experience and experimentation that I have come to prefer certain vinegar flavours with certain dishes. I have recommended particular vinegars in the recipes throughout this book but please feel free to experiment yourself. In general, the following list are the range of vinegars that I prefer to use.

☐ Wine Vinegar, both red and white
☐ Cider Vinegar, for a sweet and fruity flavour
☐ Malt Vinegar, for some chutneys and pickles
☐ Herb Vinegars, used mainly for salads
☐ Balsamic Vinegar, used more sparingly for a richer flavour

herb Vinegars

I have never been known for taking short cuts, especially when preparing food. Sometimes this is unfortunate, since I am also known for running late, but when it comes to making herb vinegars, it happens to be fortunate in terms of delivering a better taste. I know the more simple solution to flavouring vinegars with herbs is to simply add a few sprigs of the desired herbs to a bottle of vinegar. The following method is much more labour intensive, but the fruits (or vinegars) of your labour will be well worth it, not only in the short term, but in the longer term as well. Vinegars made in this way can be topped up by about $^1/_3$ each time the vinegar is used. This recipe is good for at least 4–6 top ups!

The herbs you use are a matter of your own choice. Some suggestions include rosemary, oregano, thyme, basil, fennel, parsley, sage, marjoram and, of course, tarragon, or any combination of your favourites. Keep in mind if you are mixing herbs that some have quite strong flavours that will tend to dominate herbs with less potent flavours.

1 cup (60 g/2 oz) fresh herbs
3 bay leaves, reserving 1 for garnish
10 whole black peppercorns, reserving 5 for garnish
6 whole juniper berries, reserving 2 for garnish
3 cloves garlic, reserving 1 for garnish
1 litre (32 fl oz/1$^3/_4$ pints) white or red wine vinegar
few sprigs fresh herbs to garnish
1 or 2 fresh red chillies, reserving both for garnish (optional)

1 Gently bruise the cupful of fresh herbs, perhaps in a mortar and pestle, and place the herbs into a wide necked jar big enough to hold the litre (32 fl oz/ 1$^3/_4$ pints) of vinegar. Break 2 of the bay leaves in half, lightly crack 5 of the peppercorns and 4 of the juniper berries, and slice 2 of the garlic cloves, and then place all of these in the jar with the bruised herbs.

a bit on the side

2 Pour over the vinegar and seal the jar. Allow the vinegar to stand, preferably in the sun, as this helps to warm the vinegar and extract the essential oils from the herbs and other ingredients. Leave the vinegar to flavour for about 2 weeks.

3 Strain the vinegar into a sterilised bottle. Garnish with the remaining herbs and spices, slitting the garlic clove and chillies before inserting them into the bottle. The vinegar is now ready to use as desired. Remember that you can top up the bottle with plain white or red wine vinegar when you have used about a third of the herb vinegar.

Serve in dressings or drizzled over hot steamed vegetables.

herb oils

Herb oils are made in the same way as herb vinegars, except that it is more important that the oil is warmed during the 2 week infusion time. If necessary, place the jar of oil you are infusing in a large saucepan with warm water, and heat gently, taking care not to let the water actually boil. Do this every 2 or 3 days for about 15 minutes, over the 2-week period.

1 cup (60 g/2 oz) herbs, reserving a few sprigs for garnish
10 whole black peppercorns, reserving 5 for garnish
3 cloves garlic, reserving 1 for garnish
1 litre (32 fl oz/1³/₄ pints) olive oil, your choice of extra virgin, or
pure olive oil etc, depending on your intended use
1 or 2 fresh red chillies, reserving both for garnish (optional)

See procedure for Herb Vinegars (pages 47-48).

Serve in dressings, drizzled over hot steamed vegetables, or for basting or marinating meats, fish and poultry before cooking.

Opposite: Mustard Salad Dressing and Vinaigrette Salad Dressing

mustard salad dressing

A hot, spicy dressing to add 'zing', not only to salads as I have also basted meats with this mixture while cooking on a barbecue.

3 tablespoons extra virgin olive oil
1 tablespoon seeded mustard
1-2 tablespoons lemon juice
1 teaspoon salt
1 tablespoon parsley

1 Shake all the ingredients together in a jar and use as desired. Dressings can be kept in the jar in the refrigerator for up to a week and used as desired.

Serve as a dressing for potato salad, green salads, or mixed vegetable salads.

Vinaigrette salad dressing

Most vegetables welcome this easy-to-make, light dressing.

1-2 tablespoons white wine vinegar
1 clove of garlic, sliced into quarters
$1/4$ cup (60 ml/2 fl oz) extra virgin olive oil
$1/2$ teaspoon salt
$1/4$ teaspoon freshly ground black pepper

1 Shake all the ingredients together in a jar. Remove garlic pieces, or crush them first with salt and leave them in the dressing.

Serve with green salads, mixed vegetable salads or steamed vegetables.

marinades

Marinades are a great way of tenderising the meat you want to cook as well as imparting delicious flavours and aromas during cooking. Some people prefer not to add salt, because this tends to draw the moisture out of the meat which you marinate. I have been trained to salt things before cooking, and frankly I have never found it to dry out the food.

greek-style marinade

The next best thing to having char-grilled *souvlakia* in a taverna on a Greek island is to take in the aromas of this marinade, close your eyes and imagine. When you open your eyes you may not see waves washing up onto a pebbly beach, but the flavours of your meats marinated in this will be a good interim substitute... well, nearly.

I clove garlic, crushed
¹/₄ cup (60 ml/2 fl oz) lemon juice
I teaspoon dried oregano
¹/₄ cup (60 ml/2 fl oz) olive oil
¹/₄ cup (60 g/2 oz) fresh, ripe tomatoes, very finely chopped
¹/₂ teaspoon black pepper
I small onion, grated
¹/₂ teaspoon salt (optional)

I Mix all the ingredients together in a shallow dish or bowl, then marinate desired meats or vegetables for at least 4 hours, but preferably overnight.
Use for meat (lamb, beef or chicken), seafood (octopus, fish or prawns), and vegetables (mushrooms, capsicums etc) before grilling or barbecuing.

tandoori marinade

This is an Indian-style marinade which not only tastes delicious, but adds a wonderful red colour to meats, fish or poultry. Traditionally, meats of all types which have been marinated in this mixture are then threaded onto long metal skewers and dry roasted in a tandoor oven. Unless you have a spare one lying around in the garden shed, char-grill or roast the meats you marinate on a rack in the oven, for a more than satisfactory alternative.

$1/4$ **teaspoon saffron threads, soaked in** $1/4$ **cup**
(60 ml/2 fl oz) hot water, or 1 teaspoon saffron powder
1 teaspoon ground coriander
$1/4$ **teaspoon chilli powder (optional)**
1 teaspoon cumin powder
$1/2$ **teaspoon fennel seed powder**
$1/4$ **teaspoon ground cardamom**
1 teaspoon fresh ginger, grated
2 cloves crushed garlic
$1/4$ **teaspoon ground cloves**
2 tablespoons lime or lemon juice
2 cups (500 ml/1 pint/16 fl oz) plain yoghurt
$1/2$ **teaspoon salt (optional)**

1 Combine all the ingredients in a bowl, including the saffron threads and the water in which they were soaked. Mix thoroughly.

2 Marinate desired meats or seafood in this mixture for at least 6 hours before cooking. Make sure you remove some of the excess yoghurt from the meats, as they should only be lightly coated for best results.

Use for lamb, firm-fleshed white fish fillets, or skinless chicken (chicken skin is too fatty, and the desired outcome is dry rather than oily).

Opposite: Tandoori Marinade (Chicken)

a bit on the side

asian-style marinade

This is a sweeter tasting marinade, yet it has a salty flavour from the soy sauce, and a spicy flavour from the chillies and garam masala. When cooking meats or seafood that have been marinated in this delicious mix, take extra care with the temperature of the fire, because the sugar can burn, rather than caramelise, which is the desired effect.

1 clove garlic, finely chopped
2 teaspoons fresh ginger, grated
1/4 cup (60 ml/2 fl oz) rice wine or sherry
1 teaspoon garam masala
1/3 cup (90 ml/3 fl oz) light soy sauce
1 or 2 chillies, chopped (optional)
1 teaspoon sesame oil
2 teaspoons fresh coriander root, chopped (optional).
The root of the coriander plant can be used,
and adds a wonderful flavour to this marinade.
2 teaspoons either brown sugar or honey

1 Mix all ingredients together in a shallow dish or a bowl. Marinate desired meat or seafood in this mixture for at least 4 hours, but preferably overnight.

Use as a marinade for meat (pork, beef, or chicken), and seafood (octopus, green prawns, squid, or fish).